FOUNDATIONS OF FAITH

ISAIAH 58 MOBILE TRAINING INSTITUTE

ALL NATIONS INTERNATIONAL   TERESA SKINNER
GORDON SKINNER   AGNES I NUMER

Isaiah 58 Mobile Training Institute
Foundations of Faith

ISBN:978-1-950123-30-8
Copyright © 2018 by All Nations International
All rights reserved.

Unless otherwise indicated, all Scripture quotations are taken from the Holy Bible, King James Version - Public Domain Scripture quotations marked (NLV) are taken from the Holy Bible, New Life version, copyright © Christian Literature International Scripture quotations marked (ESV) ® Bible (The Holy Bible, English Standard Version®), copyright © 2001 by Crossway, a publishing ministry of Good News Publishers. Used by permission. All rights reserved."
Scripture quotations marked (Wuest) were taken from the New Testament and Expanded Translation by Kenneth S. Wuest © 1961 by the Wm. B. Eerdmans Publishing Co. Used by permission

Authors: Rev. Agnes I. Numer, Rev. Gordon Skinner, Rev. Teresa Skinner

Special Thanks: Veronica Sanchez, Pastor Monique Handall, Aidan Handall, Angela Baron-Jeffrey, Patty Castillo

Editors: Julie Montague, Ashley Flores, Virginia Russell, Amber Lawton, Linda Vasquez, Nona Babich

Messages transcribed by: Jennene Jeffrey, Kathy Vanzandt, Karen Offerman

Artwork: Julian Peter V. Arias, Jumi Sabbagh, Teresa Skinner, Adobe Stock, www.freepik.com, Photography Director: Monique Handall

Cover Art: Julian Peter V. Arias and Eve Lorraine Rivers Trinidad

Isaiah 58 Mobile Training Institute is available for use in training programs.

For more information or to order additional copies of this manual:

Take the courses online: is58mti.org
email: allnations@as.net contact us: www.all-nations.org write to: All Nations International
PO Box 26632 Prescott Valley, AZ 86312

CONTENTS

Preface vii
Introduction ix

1. Foundations of Faith — 1
2. Who is God? — 5
   Review: Who is God? — 13
3. Why Did God Make People? — 15
   Review: Why Did God Make People? — 23
4. What Is Sin? — 25
   Review: What Is Sin? — 33
5. Who Is Jesus? — 37
   Review: Who Is Jesus? — 41
6. What Is Repentance? — 43
   Review: What Is Repentance? — 47
7. What Is Salvation? — 49
   Review: What Is Salvation? — 57
8. What Is Water Baptism? — 59
   Review: What Is Water Baptism? — 69
9. Who Is the Holy Spirit? — 71
   Review: Who Is the Holy Spirit? — 75
10. What Is the Baptism of the Holy Spirit? — 77
    Review: What Is the Baptism of the Holy Spirit? — 85
11. What Must I Do to Be Saved? — 87
12. Go Make Disciples — 91
    Review: Go Make Disciples — 99
    Review Key — 101

Acknowledgments 107
About the Author 109

PREFACE

As we travel around the world, we see pastors and leaders struggle with, "What to teach their people." Maybe they have never had Bible School training... and may never be able to afford it.

Our cry is that God will read this to you... that He will impart His Gospel to your heart, that He will train you, and that you will experience the freedom, peace power and ability to demonstrate His Love to the Nations.

May we all work together while there is time.... That He alone may be glorified.

Let Jesus take you to the Nations.....

Teresa Skinner
    Director

"And this gospel of the kingdom shall be preached in all the world for a witness unto all nations; and then shall the end come." Matthew 24:14

INTRODUCTION

In 1954, God gave Rev. Agnes I. Numer the revelation of Isaiah 58. He told her, "This is My plan, for My church, for the end of time." He showed her planes, trains, warehouses, training centers, centers of refuge, food distribution and so much more.

Rev. Numer established training centers where leaders received a vision, a hope, a plan and the principles of God's Kingdom. Those leaders passionately put these principles into practice in ministries around the globe. God has been their Jehovah Jireh.

God also showed Rev. Agnes I. Numer a school of ministry that would share these principles of His Kingdom to the nations. The Isaiah 58 Mobile Training Institute is now available in print and eBook form.

Thank you.
All Nations International

Habakkuk 2:2 (KJV) "And the Lord answered me,

and said, Write the vision, and make it plain upon tables, that he may run that readeth it. 3 For the vision is yet for an appointed time, but at the end it shall speak, and not lie: though it tarry, wait for it; because it will surely come, it will not tarry."

2 Timothy 2:2 (KJV) "And the things that thou hast heard of me among many witnesses, the same commit thou to faithful men, who shall be able to teach others also."

Rev. Agnes I. Numer, also known as the *"Mother Teresa of America"* passed away July 17, 2010 at 95 years of age. She has leaves behind a tremendous legacy.

We dedicate this manual:
To those who wanted to know... but never had a teacher.
To those who looked for the vision... so that they could run with it.
To those who want to know "What's Next?"
To those who knew they were teachers... but did not know what to teach.
To those who are looking for Christ in Us the Hope of Glory!
May this manual reveal to you Jesus Christ and
May the peace that He has ordained for you be with you always.

1

FOUNDATIONS OF FAITH

When we attempt to explain who God is, we often encounter a problem: In today's world, many people go to church, but they do not realize that the Infinite Being that they serve is not some imaginary, distant creature. Instead, He is a Loving Creator who cares for each and every single one of us and who demonstrates His Love in very real, very tangible ways.

As a pastor, you may also experience people who resist the fact that God is real and that we are created in His Image. God appears in the Old Testament as the God of Abraham, Isaac, and Jacob. He is the God who answers by fire. He is the God who is unchanging and forever. He is the King of all Kings.

Ultimately, the only way to get to know Him is to know Him for who He is - not who we want Him to be.

Therefore, in this short introductory lesson, we will provide you with ways to introduce people to God and His person. The outline that we have provided will give you short videos that help to explain the biblical principles on which you may build your discussion with your students. It is our hope that as you use this basic outline God will reveal Himself to you.

Being willing to discover who God really is matters. Sometimes, we think that God is created in our image, and we fail to realize that we were created in His image. God appears in the Old Testament as the God of Abraham, Isaac, and Jacob. He is also known as the God who answers by fire.

It is important that we realize who God is and that He wants to bring us back to the relationship and fellowship that He had with us in the beginning, in the Garden of Eden. He desires that we know Him personally and intimately. Just as He walked with Adam and Abraham, so does this Incredible Loving Father desire that you and I would know Him as He is.

As we discover in Psalm 103:6, we learn that God "made known His ways to Moses His acts to the children of Israel."

By studying the statements and questions below, we can begin to allow God to reveal Himself to you. In this section, you will learn the answers to the following questions. It is our hope that as you find the answer, **you will ...
know God.**

Some questions we will answer:

- Who is God?
- Where does He live?
- What color is God?
- Who did God choose to represent Himself?
- How did God prepare the Jewish people?
- Why is this important to us?

2
WHO IS GOD?

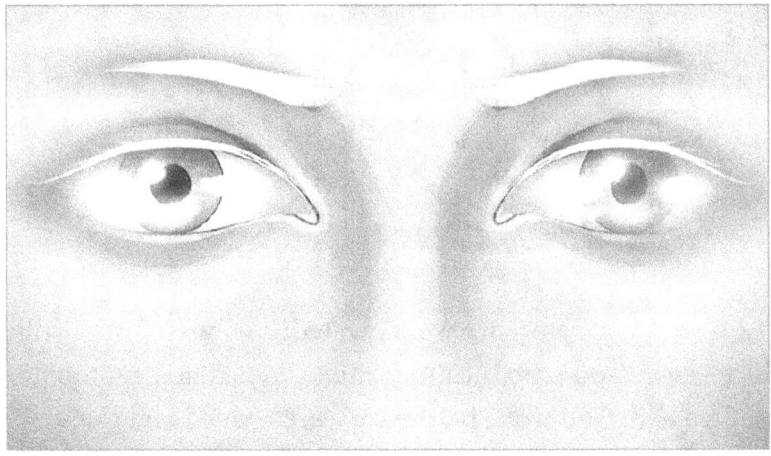

In today's world many go to church and do not realize the Infinite Being that they serve. We think God is created in our image and do not realize that **we are created in His image.** God appears in the Old Testament as the God of Abraham, Isaac and Jacob and the God who answers by fire.

Let's get to know Him for who He is... not who we want Him to be.

Study the statements and questions below and **allow God to reveal Himself to you.**

Who is God?

Watch Video: Click to watch Creation Genesis Video
or go to: is58mti.org and under Categories click Resources

God was... before we were created. God was, is, and will be forever. God is an Infinite Being who had no beginning and no end. God was... before we were created and He will be here long after we die. As we can read in Genesis, God made, He created everything — heaven and earth, and all living things. God also made man in His own image.

Genesis 1:1, In the beginning God created the heaven and the earth.

He made man in His Image. Man did not make the image of God.

Take a few minutes to **view the Creation Genesis video.** As we view this video see the greatness of God's creation and how that He made the world the stars the planets the water, God made you and He made me.

Genesis 1: 26 And God said, Let us make man in our image, after our likeness: and let them have dominion over the fish of the sea, and over the fowl of the air, and over the cattle, and over all the earth, and over every creeping thing that creepeth upon the earth. 27 So God created man in his [own] image, in the image of God created he him; male and female created he them.

Man was created in God's image. What is His image? what is His personality how does God feel about His people? How does God feel about you?

God created all things for His pleasure. He created you and I for His pleasure. God is so great and yet He is great enough to live inside of our hearts. He will take the time to hear our thoughts and prayers.

God is... jealous over you.

God wants the best for you. He knows that sin causes death and destruction this is why He gave commands of how to live. The Bible is like an instruction manual. It is His word written for man. for man to understand His ways and His commands.

Exodus 34:14 For thou shalt worship no other god: for the LORD, whose name [is] Jealous, [is] a jealous God:

God is... merciful, gracious, slow to anger, abundant in loving kindness and truth...

Exodus 34:6 And the LORD passed by before him, and proclaimed, The LORD, The LORD God, merciful and gracious, longsuffering, and abundant in goodness and truth,

Psalm 145:8 The LORD [is] gracious, and full of compassion; slow to anger, and of great mercy.

WHERE does He live?

God lives... in heaven and in our hearts.

When we ask Jesus to forgive us of our sins and ask Him to come into our hearts He will. God has made us for His pleasure and His glory, He wants a very close relationship with us this is why He made us in the beginning.

Ephesians 2:21-22 (NLV)

21 Christ keeps this building together and it is growing into a holy building for the Lord. 22 You are also being put together as a part of this building because God lives in you by His Spirit.

God has... His own Kingdom and His own Nationality.

A lot of times people think God is like their Father or their friends. He is not. God has His own culture, His own way of expressing Himself. We do not and cannot control Him. He is God.

Luke 11:2 And he said unto them, When ye pray, say, Our Father which art in heaven, Hallowed be thy name. Thy kingdom come. Thy will be done, as in heaven, so in earth.

John 18:36 Jesus answered, My kingdom is not of this world:... but now is my kingdom not from hence.

WHAT color is God?

Watch Video: "What Color is God?"
 or go to: is58mti.org and under Categories click Resources

God is... light - light is the presence of all colors.
1 John 1:5 This then is the message which we have heard of him, and declare unto you, that God is light, and in him is no darkness at all.

God is not... white, brown, yellow or black.

God is... all colors – ALL men are made in His image.

When we see pictures of God they are only ideas that man has come up with. God's word says that He created man in His image. He did not say which man, but all men are created by God and in His image.

Genesis 1:27 So God created man in his own image, in the image of God created he him; male and female created he them.

WHO did God choose to represent Himself?

Historically **God chose...** Israel, the Jewish people. God prepared them for more than 4,000 years to bring His Son Jesus, the Messiah to the earth.

Deuteronomy 7:6 For thou [art] an holy people unto the LORD thy God: the LORD thy God hath chosen thee to be a special people unto himself, above all people that [are] upon the face of the earth.

Today, ***God chooses...*** *those that have ears to hear*

1 Peter 2:9 But ye [are] a chosen generation, a royal priesthood, an holy nation, a peculiar (or purchased) people; that ye should shew forth the praises of him who hath called you out of darkness into his marvelous light: 10 Which in time past [were] not a people, but [are] now the people of God: which had not obtained mercy, but now have obtained mercy.

HOW did God prepare the Jewish people?

God showed... *them Himself.*

God spent time with Adam and Eve in the garden of Eden. He taught them how to care for the garden and how to care for themselves. As we read the book of Exodus we see that God stayed with the Israelites daily, guiding them by a cloud during the day and a fire by night. For more than forty years God fed them from His hand until they reached the Promised Land.

God taught the Jewish people how to story tell until they were able to write down their history. He showed them that it was important to hand down His ways and commandments to their children and their children's children.

God taught them morals – what is right and what is wrong.

It took God more than 4,000 years to prepare Israel for Jesus to come to them.

- Adam to Abraham - 2,000 years *(20 generations)*
- Abraham to Jesus - 2,000 years *(55 generations)*
- Jesus to Present - 2,000 years

Matthew 1:17
So all the generations from Abraham to David [are] fourteen generations; and from David until the carrying away into Babylon [are] fourteen generations; and from the carrying away into Babylon unto Christ [are] fourteen generations.

WHY is this important to us?

It is important that we realize who God is and that He wants to bring us back to the relationship and fellowship that He had with us in the beginning, in the Garden of Eden. He desires that we know Him personally and intimately, just as He walked with Adam and Abraham, so does this incredible being desire that you and I would know Him as He is.

Psalm 103:6 He made known His ways to Moses His acts to the children of Israel. That we may... **know God.**

REVIEW: WHO IS GOD?

1. Some people see God as an imaginary, distant creature.
a. True
b. False

2. We must _____ God for who He is – not who we _____ Him to be.

3. Sometimes, we _____ that God is created in our image, and we _____ to _____ that we were created in His _____.

4. God was... before we were created. God was, is, and will be forever.
a. True
b. False

5. The Bible is like an instruction manual. It is His word written for man to

a. know where we can get away with sin
b. understand His ways and His commands
c. live life our way and still get to heaven.

6. God _____ the Jewish people by _____ them Himself.

7. God has... His own Kingdom and His own Nationality.
a. True
b. False

8. What color is God?
a. Black
b. White
c. Yellow
d. Green
e. Red
f. Light
g. Dark

3
WHY DID GOD MAKE PEOPLE?

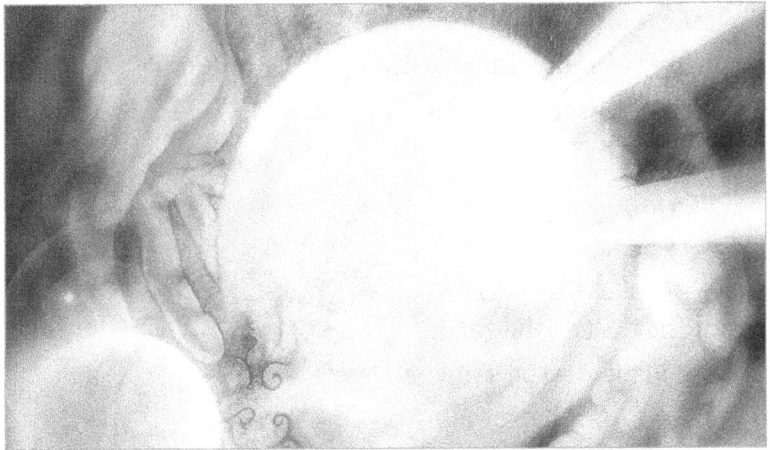

God has everything, can do anything and is so complete in Himself that He does not need anything, so why would He create people?

Since God knows everything, He knew His beautiful people, Adam and Eve, were going to sin. He knew His perfect creation would be damaged by the death and destructiveness which come as direct consequences of living outside of God. So why would He still make people?

God made people because He wanted to have a people who freely chose to know Him, talk with Him and live forever together with Him. God's great Father Heart of Love wanted to share with a people who were His. He knew He would have a people who would love Him and live with Him forever. He knew that if He had a few people who came to know how amazingly beautiful He is they would show others about Him.

Lev 26:12 And I will walk among you, and will be your God, and ye shall be my people.

Isa 43:21 This people have I formed for myself; they shall shew forth my praise.

Study the following questions and allow God to reveal to you why He created people.

HOW did God make people?

Man was formed by God out of the dust of the earth. He was made in God's image to have dominion over all living things, to have children and to subdue the earth.

Genesis 1:26 And God said, Let us make man in our image, after our likeness: and let them have dominion over the fish of the sea, and over the fowl of the air, and over the cattle, and over all the earth, and over every creeping thing that creepeth upon the earth.

So God created man in his own image, in the image of God created he him; male and female created he them.

Genesis 2:7 And the LORD God formed man of the dust of the ground, and breathed into his nostrils the breath of life; and man became a living soul.

God saw Adam was alone, so He made a woman, Eve, out of a rib he took from Adam's side.

Genesis 2:18 And the LORD God said, It is not good that the man should be alone; I will make him an help meet for him.

Genesis 2:21 And the LORD God caused a deep sleep to fall upon Adam, and he slept: and he took one of his ribs and closed up the flesh instead thereof; 22 And the rib, which the LORD God had taken from man, made he a woman, and brought her unto the man.

HOW are we created in God's Image?

When someone says, "You are just like your Father", they are saying that you talk, walk, think and act just like your Father, or that you have special abilities like he does. When God created us, He gave us special abilities and characteristics like He has.

We have spiritual abilities to know God, to talk with Him and to be aware of His presence.

We have a free will – we can choose. **We are creative** – we can create.

We have intelligence – we can think, learn, and understand.

We have authority – we can rule (subdue, take dominion, organize)

WHAT was the Garden of Eden?

Imagine a place – the most beautiful garden or park where there is no pain, suffering or torment. Everything you need to eat grows naturally there for you. The animals get along peacefully. No one fights or is angry; there are no bad attitudes and no unkind words. Together, God and His people walked and talked in the garden when the evenings became cool.

Everything was perfect.

This is what God made in the beginning – for the people He loved.

Genesis 2:8 And the LORD God planted a garden eastward in Eden; and there he put the man whom he had formed. 9 And out of the ground made the LORD God to grow every tree that is pleasant to the sight, and good for food; the tree of life also in the midst of the garden, and the tree of knowledge of good and evil.

WHAT was the One Single Don't?

DO NOT eat of the tree of the knowledge of good and evil.

Rebellion, disobedience, self-will, lying, sneakiness, blame, shame, distrust, suspicion, so many sins were stirred up by the only "don't" God gave to Adam and Eve. We really don't need a lot of laws and rules to stir up our sin nature, we really do not like being told what to do and we do love to **"do our own thing our own way"** instead of God's way.

Genesis 2:16 And the LORD God commanded the man, saying, Of every tree of the garden thou mayest freely eat: 17 But of the tree of the knowledge of good and evil, thou shalt not eat of it: for in the day that thou eatest thereof thou shalt surely die.

WHO is God's One Enemy?

God has one enemy, he is evil and he hates God and hates His people. He does not want God to have a people who will love Him. This enemy will do everything in his wicked power to stop God's plan. This enemy's name is Satan or the Devil. He came to the Garden of Eden in the disguise of a serpent to plant suggestions in the minds of Adam and Eve. His tools twisted the truth, accused God, deceived Eve and told lies. His purpose was to steal, kill and destroy.

Genesis 3:1 Now the serpent was more subtle than any beast of the field which the LORD God had made. And he said unto the woman, Yea, hath God said, Ye shall not eat of every tree of the garden? 2 And the woman said unto the serpent, We may eat of the fruit of the trees of the garden: 3 But of the fruit of the tree which is in the midst of the garden, God hath said, Ye shall not eat of it, neither shall ye touch it, lest ye die. 4 And the serpent said unto the woman, Ye shall not surely die: 5 For God doth know that in the day ye eat thereof, then your eyes shall be opened, and ye shall be as gods, knowing good and evil. 6 And when the woman saw that the tree was good for food, and that it was pleasant to the eyes, and a tree to be desired to make one wise, she took of the fruit thereof, and did eat, and gave also unto her husband with her; and he did eat. 7 And the eyes of them both were opened, and they knew that they were naked; and they sewed fig leaves together, and made themselves aprons. 8 And they heard the voice of the LORD God walking in the garden in the cool of the day: and Adam and his wife hid themselves from the presence of the LORD God amongst the trees of the garden. 9 And the LORD God called unto Adam, and said unto him, Where art thou? 10 And he said, I heard thy voice in the garden, and I was afraid, because I was naked; and I hid myself. 11 And he said, Who told thee that thou wast naked? Hast thou eaten of the tree, whereof I commanded thee that thou shouldest not eat? 12 And the man said, The woman whom thou gavest to be with me, she gave me of the tree, and I did eat. 13 And the LORD God said unto the woman, What is this that thou hast done? And the woman said, The serpent beguiled me, and I did eat.

One Sin Many Consequences

Adam and Eve suffered so many consequences or "wages" for their sin.

Genesis 3:16 Unto the woman he said, I will greatly multiply thy sorrow and thy conception; in sorrow thou shalt bring forth children; and thy desire shall be to thy husband, and he shall rule over thee. 17 And unto Adam he said, Because thou hast hearkened unto the voice of thy wife, and hast eaten of the tree, of which I commanded thee, saying, Thou shalt not eat of it: cursed is the ground for thy sake; in sorrow shalt thou eat of it all the days of thy life; 18 Thorns also and thistles shall it bring forth to thee; and thou shalt eat the herb of the field; 19 In the sweat of thy face shalt thou eat bread, till thou return unto the ground; for out of it wast thou taken: for dust thou art, and unto dust shalt thou return.

Man no longer walked nor talked with God. Trouble and difficulties came from every side. The world became an ugly place to live – because of sin.

God told them all of these things would happen if they disobeyed His one "don't". These things are called "Death".

NOW men are born with the tendency to sin
...it is in our DNA.

Romans 5:12 Wherefore, as by one man sin entered into the world, and death by sin; and so death passed upon all men, for that all have sinned.

People have lost their "God breathed" characteristics, they have lost the strength to create or to choose what is right and they have become slaves to sin. People are still separated from the God who made them to fellowship with Him. People are still being deceived and lied to by the devil who is still making sin look appealing and blaming God for "holding out on us".

WHERE is Our Hope?

God's plan is greater than our weakness and disobedience, He is wiser than the Devil who steals and destroys. God's plan is stronger than Sin itself. Our Hope points to a Savior, a solution, a repairing of our broken relationship.

God's son's life and death will bring man back into the right relationship with God the Father if we accept Jesus,

God's provision, and again – become His people and let Him become our God.

GOD WANTS YOU to Become One of His People. God loves you and wants you to know Him and learn His ways. He will save you

from the devil's lies and the bondages of sin. **God wants to restore** to you His special characteristics that He gave to Adam. **God wants to bring you back** into "the image of God". You will again be one of His people and **He will be your God.** You will learn to know Him, walk with Him and talk with Him.

REVIEW: WHY DID GOD MAKE PEOPLE?

1. God made people because:
a. He was lonely
b. He lacked someone to love Him
c. He wanted a people who would freely choose to live with Him forever
d. The angels were not able to satisfy His need for love

2. How did God make people?
a. He spoke man into existence
b. He formed man out of dust
c. He gave angels human bodies
d. He caused them to evolve from lower life forms

3. To be created in God's image means:
a. We have a free will to choose like He does
b. We have the ability to create like He does

4. What purpose did Satan have when he deceived Eve?

a. To steal her relationship with God
b. To destroy God's plan for man
c. To separate man from God
d. All of the above

5. What are the consequences of man's sin
a. Man is now born with a tendency to sin
b. Man became a slave to sin
c. The beautifully created world became a difficult place to live
d. All of the above

6. What hope is there for man?
a. By accepting God's Son as our savior we can again become His people
b. If we try harder and live right God might again accept us
c. If we do all of the right things we might earn His friendship
d. By reading and following the Bible to the best of our ability

4

WHAT IS SIN?

Isaiah 59:2 But your iniquities (sins) have separated between you and your God, and your sins have hid his face from you, that he will not hear. Scriptures tell us that sin separates us from God.

In our world today many do not want to face sin, they want to think that what we are doing is right and do not want to change. But since the God of Abraham, Isaac and Jacob says that sin separates us from Him, we must seek His face as to what He says is sin and do what He says we should do about it. Then we will see His Face and hear His words.

Study the statements and questions below and allow God to show you what He calls sin, how He says it will affect you and what we should do about sin.

Sin is doing what we were not created to do:
Is what I am doing a sin? Ask yourself these questions:

- Does it make you grow old faster?
- Does it make you sick or unhealthy?
- Do you have to justify it? Or constantly tell yourself it is right?
- Did you feel guilty when you started doing it?
- Do you have to keep yourself from doing it too much?
- Is it sin?

Romans 6:23 For the wages of sin is death; but the gift of God is eternal life through Jesus Christ our Lord.

WHAT does God call Sin?

The 10 Commandments

> Exodus 20:1 And God spake all these words, saying,
>   2 I [am] the LORD thy God, which have brought thee out of the land of Egypt, out of the house of bondage.
>   3 Thou shalt have no other gods before me.

4 Thou shalt not make unto thee any graven image, or any likeness [of anything] that [is] in heaven above, or that [is] in the earth beneath, or that [is] in the water under the earth:

5 Thou shalt not bow down thyself to them, nor serve them: for I the LORD thy God [am] a jealous God, visiting the iniquity of the fathers upon the children unto the third and fourth [generation] of them that hate me;

6 And shewing mercy unto thousands of them that love me, and keep my commandments.

7 Thou shalt not take the name of the LORD thy God in vain; for the LORD will not hold him guiltless that taketh his name in vain.

8 Remember the sabbath day, to keep it holy. 9 Six days shalt thou labor, and do all thy work:

10 But the seventh day [is] the sabbath of the LORD thy God: [in it] thou shalt not do any work, thou, nor thy son, nor thy daughter, thy manservant, nor thy maidservant, nor thy cattle, nor thy stranger that [is] within thy gates:

11 For [in] six days the LORD made heaven and earth, the sea, and all that in them [is], and rested the seventh day: wherefore the LORD blessed the sabbath day, and hallowed it.

12 Honour thy father and thy mother: that thy days may be long upon the land which the LORD thy God giveth thee.

13 Thou shalt not kill. 14 Thou shalt not commit adultery. 15 Thou shalt not steal. 16 Thou shalt not bear false witness against thy neighbor.

17 Thou shalt not covet thy neighbor's house, thou shalt not covet thy neighbor's wife, nor his manservant,

nor his maidservant, nor his ox, nor his ass, nor any thing that [is] thy neighbor's.

Sin separates us from God. God wants to bring us back to the relationship and fellowship that He had with us in the beginning in the Garden of Eden.

Matthew 6:24 "No one can serve two masters; for either he will hate the one and love the other, or else he will be loyal to the one and despise the other. You cannot serve God and mammon.

Num 15:37 And the LORD spake unto Moses, saying, 38 Speak unto the children of Israel, and bid them that they make them fringes in the borders of their garments throughout their generations, and that they put upon the fringe of the borders a ribband of blue: 39 And it shall be unto you for a fringe, that ye may look upon it, and remember all the commandments of the LORD, and do them; and that ye seek not after your own heart and your own eyes, after which ye use to go a whoring: 40 That ye may remember, and do all my commandments, and be holy unto your God. 41 I [am] the LORD your God, which brought you out of the land of Egypt, to be your God: I [am] the LORD your God.

WHAT are we supposed to do about SIN?

- Flee from Sin.
- Submit to God.
- Resist the devil.
- Draw near to God.

- Cleanse your hands.
- Purify your hearts.
- Make up your mind.
- Repent from sin.
- Humble yourselves before God.
- Flee from Sin.

1 Corinthians 6:18 Flee fornication. Every sin that a man doeth is without the body; but he that committeth fornication sinneth against his own body.

Submit to God. Submit: Yield to God's wisdom and direction.

James 4:7 Therefore submit to God. Resist the devil and he will flee from you. 8 Draw near to God and He will draw near to you. Cleanse your hands, you sinners; and purify your hearts, you double-minded. 9 Lament and mourn and weep! Let your laughter be turned to mourning and your joy to gloom. 10 Humble yourselves in the sight of the Lord, and He will lift you up.

WHAT do we do if we SIN?

We must look at our sin the way God sees it; we cannot excuse it. We must Repent.

What is Repentance?

Repentance is looking at the sin we have committed... God's way. When we do, we become sorry for what we have done and we turn from it. Sometimes... we have to run from it.

2 Corinthians 7:10 (NLV) The sorrow that God uses

makes people sorry for their sin and leads them to turn from sin so they can be saved from the punishment of sin. We should be happy for that kind of sorrow, but the sorrow of this world brings death.

Human Regret is not Repentance

Hebrews 12:16 Lest there [be] any fornicator, or profane person, as Esau, who for one morsel of meat sold his birthright. 17 For ye know how that afterward, when he would have inherited the blessing, he was rejected: for he found no place of repentance, though he sought it carefully with tears.

WHAT if we are weak to sin?

The reason why God sent His only Son, Jesus to die on the cross for us is because we ARE weak to sin. The process of truly being born again creates a new nature within us and through that nature God gives us power over sin. This is God's pleasure.

Matthew 5:6 Blessed are those who hunger and thirst for righteousness, For they shall be filled.

Matthew 5:8 Blessed are the pure in heart, For they shall see God.

God will work with those who will work with Him.

Luke 12:32 Fear not, little flock; for it is your Father's good pleasure to give you the kingdom.

Philippians 2:12 Wherefore, my beloved, as ye have always obeyed, not as in my presence only, but now much more in my absence, work out your own salvation with fear and trembling. 13 For it is God which worketh in you both to will and to do of his good pleasure.

Isaiah 26:12 LORD, thou wilt ordain peace for us: for thou also hast wrought all our works in us. 13 O LORD our God, [other] lords beside thee have had dominion over us: [but] by thee only will we make mention of thy name. 14 [They are] dead, they shall not live; [they are] deceased, they shall not rise: therefore hast thou visited and destroyed them, and made all their memory to perish.

WHAT does the Bible call sin?

Galatians 5:19 Now the works of the flesh are manifest, which are these; Adultery, fornication, uncleanness, lasciviousness, 20 Idolatry, witchcraft, hatred, variance, emulations, wrath, strife, seditions, heresies, 21 Envyings, murders, drunkenness, revellings, and such like: of the which I tell you before, as I have also told you in time past, that they which do such things shall not inherit the kingdom of God.

Amplified Bible Version

Galatians 5:19 Now the doings practices) of the flesh are clear obvious): they are immorality, impurity, indecency, 20 Idolatry, sorcery, enmity, strife, jealousy, anger ill temper), selfishness, divisions dissensions), party spirit factions, sects with peculiar opinions, heresies), 21 Envy, drunkenness, carousing, and the like. I warn you beforehand, just as I did previously, that those who do such things shall not inherit the kingdom of God. Amplified Bible (AMP)

SIN is also NOT DOING what we were created to do

In our lives, God gives us commands and instructions to follow. This is for our own well-being. It is to make us into the person He created us to be. It is also for the benefit of others. When we do not obey God it is sin.

Read the Parable of the Wise and Foolish Virgins in Matthew 25:1-13

Deut 30:20 That thou mayest love the LORD thy God, [and] that thou mayest obey his voice, and that thou mayest cleave unto him: for he [is] thy life, and the length of thy days: that thou mayest dwell in the land which the LORD sware unto thy fathers, to Abraham, to Isaac, and to Jacob, to give them.

Jonah 1:1 Now the word of the LORD came unto Jonah the son of Amittai, saying, 2 Arise, go to Nineveh, that great city, and cry against it; for their wickedness is come up before me. 3 But Jonah rose up to flee unto Tarshish from the presence of the LORD, and went down to Joppa; and he found a ship going to Tarshish: so he paid the fare thereof, and went down into it, to go with them unto Tarshish from the presence of the LORD.

REVIEW: WHAT IS SIN?

1. Sin is doing what we are created to do.
a. True
b. False

2. Sin is doing what we not created to do. Sin will make us _____ or unhealthy.

3. Thou shall not _____ unto thee any _____ _____, or any _____ that is in heaven above or that is earth _____ or that is in the water or the earth

4. Thou shalt not take the _____ of the LORD thy _____ in vain; for the LORD will not hold him _____ that taketh his name in _____.

5. "And it shall be unto you for a fringe, that ye may look upon it, and _____ _____ the commandments of the LORD, and _____ _____; and that ye _____ _____

after your _____ heart and your own eyes, after which ye use to go a whoring:"

6. We must flee from sin.
a. True
b. False

7. We should get on the devil's side.
a. True
b. False

8. We must draw near to God.
a. True
b. False

9. We should resist the devil.
a. True
b. False

10. We should submit or yield to God's wisdom and direction.
a. True
b. False

11. What is NOT repentance?
a. humbling yourself before the Lord
b. turning from sin
c. human regret
d. asking the Lord for forgiveness

12. What the Bible calls sin: "Now the works of the flesh are

manifest, which are these; Adultery, _____, uncleanness, _____, idolatry, witchcraft, _____, variance, emulations, _____, _____, seditions, heresies, _____, murders, _____, revellings, and such like: of the which I tell you before, as I have also told you in time past, that they which _____ _____ _____ shall not _____ the kingdom of God."

13. Sin is also not doing what we were _____ to do.

14. Repentance is:
a. running from sin
b. becoming sorry for what we have done, and we turn away from it
c. we ignore the correction and continue sinning
d. 1 and 2 is how we repent

5
WHO IS JESUS?

We now understand that **sin separates us from God.** We have all sinned and now what can we do? This separation is very real.

Sometimes we feel that separation and that we must go on a journey to find God. We need something to happen so we can come back into that relationship with this Incredible Infinite Being, the God of Abraham, Isaac and Jacob.

Study the statements and questions below and allow Jesus to reveal Himself to you.

WHY are we separated from God?

God, the Creator of the Universe Walked with Adam and Eve in the Garden Adam sinned. Adam's sin separated him and all of his descendants from God. *So simple and yet so amazing.*

Genesis 3:23 Therefore the LORD God sent him (Adam) forth from the garden of Eden, to till the ground from whence he was taken. 24 So he drove out the man; and he placed at the east of the garden of Eden, Cherubims and a flaming sword which turned every way, to keep the way of the tree of life.

Adam and Eve became cursed and alone.

It cost the life with the shedding of blood so that our sins might be forgiven. God called this a sacrifice.

Leviticus 4:35 And he shall take away all the fat thereof, as the fat of the lamb is taken away from the sacrifice of the peace offerings; and the priest shall burn them upon the altar, according to the offerings made by fire unto the LORD: and the priest shall make an atonement for his sin that he hath committed, and it shall be forgiven him.

Many religions around the world have ceremonies that include a sacrifice of shedding of blood to forgive our sins. It is amazing that people who have never heard about this God, know that our sins have separated us from something.

WHO is Jesus?

Jesus is the Son of God

John 3:16 For God so loved the world, that he gave his only begotten Son, that whosoever believeth in him should not perish, but have everlasting life.

Jesus is Emmanuel – God on Earth Matthew 1:23 Behold, a virgin shall be with child, and shall bring forth a son, and they shall call his name Emmanuel, which being interpreted is, God with us.

Jesus became Man to Save Man

Matthew 1:21 "She will bear a Son; and you shall call His name Jesus, for He will save His people from their sins."

God sent Jesus to become **"The Ultimate Sacrifice."**

Jesus became the Sacrifice for Our Sins

John 1:29 The next day John seeth Jesus coming unto him, and saith, Behold the Lamb of God, which taketh away the sin of the world.

Sacrifices for man's sin had to be made once a year. Jesus was the Ultimate Sacrifice because when He died on the cross no other sacrifice is needed. Jesus not only washes away our sin but cleanses us from all past, present and future sins and He works in our hearts that we may not continue to live in sin.

1John 1:7 But if we walk in the light, as he is in the light, we have fellowship one with another, and the blood of Jesus Christ his Son cleanseth us from all sin.

JESUS brought us back to the Father.

John 20:17 Jesus saith unto her, Touch me not; for I am not yet ascended to my Father: but go to my brethren, and say unto them, I ascend unto my Father, and your Father; and [to] my God, and your God.

Jesus' Ultimate Sacrifice makes Him Our Savior

Matthew 1:21 "She will bear a son; and you shall call his name Jesus, for he will save his people from their sins."

John 1:1 In the beginning was the Word, and the Word was with God, and the Word was God. 2 The same was in the beginning with God. 3 All things were made by him; and without him was not any thing made that was made. 4 In him was life; and the life was the light of men. 5 And the light shineth in darkness; and the darkness comprehended it not. 6 There was a man sent from God, whose name was John. 7 The same came for a witness, to bear witness of the Light, that all men through him might believe. 8 He was not that Light, but was sent to bear witness of that Light. 9 That was the true Light, which lighteth every man that cometh into the world. 10 He was in the world, and the world was made by him, and the world knew him not. 11He came unto his own, and his own received him not. 12 But as many as received him, to them gave he power to become the sons of God, even to them that believe on his name: 13 Which were born, not of blood, nor of the will of the flesh, nor of the will of man, but of God. 14 And the Word was made flesh, and dwelt among us, (and we beheld his glory, the glory as of the only begotten of the Father,) full of grace and truth.

REVIEW: WHO IS JESUS?

1. Jesus is the _____ of God.

2. Jesus is Emmanuel - God on _____.

3. Jesus became _____ to _____ man.

4. God sent Jesus to become "the _____ sacrifice for our _____."

5. But if we _____ in the light, as _____ is in the light, we have _____ one with another, and the _____ of Jesus Christ his Son _____ us from all sin.

6. Jesus' ultimate sacrifice makes Him our _____.

7. But as many as received him, to them gave he _____ to become the _____ of God, even to them that _____ on his name:

8. And the Word was made _____, and dwelt among us, (and we beheld his glory, the glory as of the only begotten of the Father,) full of grace and truth.

6
WHAT IS REPENTANCE?

We now realize we have a problem. Sin has separated us from God. The God of Abraham, Isaac and Jacob sent His Son to be our Ultimate Sacrifice.
How do we get to where God is taking us?
Study the statements and questions below and allow Jesus to show you the path to God.

WHAT is the problem?

Genesis 3:22 And the LORD God said, Behold, the man is become as one of us, to know good and evil: and now, lest he put forth his hand, and take also of the tree of life, and eat, and live for ever: 23 Therefore the LORD God sent him forth from the garden of Eden, to till the ground from whence he was taken. 24 So he drove out the man; and he placed at the east of the garden of Eden Cherubims, and a flaming sword which turned every way, to keep the way of the tree of life.

Rom 3:23 For all have sinned, and come short of the glory of God;

Rom 5:12 Wherefore, as by one man sin entered into the world, and death by sin; and so death passed upon all men, for that all have sinned:

WHAT is the Solution?

Repentance - John the Baptist came first to prepare the world for Jesus:

Acts 19:4 Then said Paul, John verily baptized with the baptism of repentance, saying unto the people, that they should believe on him which should come after him, that is, on Christ Jesus.

HUMAN REGRET is not Repentance

2 Corinthians 7:10 (NLV) The sorrow that God uses makes people sorry for their sin and leads them to turn from sin so they can be saved from the punishment of sin. We should be

happy for that kind of sorrow, but the sorrow of this world brings death..

A sample of regret without repentance:

Matt 27:3 Then Judas, which had betrayed him, when he saw that he was condemned, repented himself, and brought again the thirty pieces of silver to the chief priests and elders, 4 Saying, I have sinned in that I have betrayed the innocent blood. And they said, What is that to us? see thou to that. 5 And he cast down the pieces of silver in the temple, and departed, and went and hanged himself.

Hebrews 12:16 Lest there [be] any fornicator, or profane person, as Esau, who for one morsel of meat sold his birthright. 17 For ye know how that afterward, when he would have inherited the blessing, he was rejected: for he found no place of repentance, though he sought it carefully with tears.

GODLY SORROW – Godly sorrow leads to doing something about the situation.

Matthew 21:29 He answered and said, I will not: but afterward he repented, and went. 30 And he came to the second, and said likewise. And he answered and said, I [go], sir: and went not. 31 Whether of them twain did the will of [his] father? They say unto him, The first...

2 Corinthians 7:10 (NLV) 10 The sorrow that God uses makes people sorry for their sin and leads them to turn from sin so they can be saved from the punishment of sin. We should be happy for that kind of sorrow, but the sorrow of this world brings death. 11 See how this sorrow God allowed you to have has worked in you. You had a desire to be free of that sin I wrote about. You were angry about it. You were afraid. You wanted to do something

about it. In every way you did what you could to make it right.

Matthew 5:6 Blessed are those who hunger and thirst for righteousness, For they shall be filled.

Matthew 5:8 Blessed are the pure in heart, For they shall see God.

Do you have something that you would like to repent from? Have you asked Jesus the Ultimate Sacrifice to come into your heart and give you a new life? Have you found yourself ignoring sin and doing what you think is right and not looking to what the God of Abraham, Isaac, and Jacob says is right? Maybe you would like to pray and ask Him for forgiveness and begin that new life right now.

If this describes what you are feeling in your heart right now, go to "WHAT MUST I DO TO BE SAVED" read the short chapter, pray to God and confess all of your sins to Him, ask Him to forgive you, ask Him for a new life in Him. Seek out a mature believer who can help you as you walk in this new walk.

REVIEW: WHAT IS REPENTANCE?

1. For all have _____ and come _____ of the _____ of God.

2. How do we get to where God wants to take us?
a. by trying to stop doing that which is keeping us from God
b. by serving food to the homeless shelter
c. by going to church twice a week
d. by repenting of what has separated (our sin) us from God

3. Human regret is the same as repentance from our sins, it saves us from the punishment of sin.

4. Godly _____ leads to _____ something about the situation.

5. "He answered and said, I will not: but afterward he _____, and went."

6. "Blessed are the _____ in heart, for they shall _____ God."

7. Have you found yourself _____ sin and doing what _____ _____ is right and not looking to what the _____ of Abraham, Isaac and Jacob says is _____? Maybe you would like to _____ and ask Him for _____ and begin that _____ _____ right now.

7
WHAT IS SALVATION?

Salvation – the gift that comes through accepting Jesus Christ the "Ultimate Sacrifice" who brings us back to the Father, back to who we were created to be and brings us to the place where we are spending eternity with our Creator.

Salvation starts with us. God already gave the Gift, Jesus

already died and rose again, now it is up to us. What will we do with this gift?

Study the statements and questions below and allow God to reveal His Gift of Salvation to you.

WHY do we need Salvation?

God, the Creator of the Universe -
  Walked with Adam and Eve in the Garden.
  Adam sinned.
  Adam's sin separated him and all of his descendants from God.
  Genesis 3:24 So he drove out the man; and he placed at the east of the garden of Eden Cherubims, and a flaming sword which turned every way, to keep the way of the tree of life.
  Ezekiel 36:17 Son of man, when the house of Israel dwelt in their own land, they defiled it by their own way and by their doings: their way was before me as the uncleanness of a removed woman.

WHAT happens during Salvation?

When Jesus died on the cross, He took the Sin into the grave, He went right into hell, and took the keys that separate us from God, right away from Satan and Jesus won the battle right there for you and I. That's how Salvation starts and now it's up to us to receive it.

God has offered us a new life:

Excerpt from "A New Birth and Foundation" by Rev. Agnes I. Numer

In Ezekiel 36 God tells about the New Birth, what is that New Birth?

God says, I'll take you out from among the heathen and take the heathen out of you. I will take the adultery out of you. He said I will place a new spirit within you. What is that spirit? The spirit that Adam and Eve had before they sinned.

This is the new spirit given back to us when we are born again. What does He mean? He does not mean that we will be born in the flesh again, He means that He will put a New Spirit inside of us a New Beginning, a New Birth. We are going to be birthed back to the Garden of Eden, brought back to that time when they were without sin and they had fellowship with Him.

He said I'll take it all out of you, I will give you a new spirit and I will put within you a new heart. He had to take the old heart out and He put a new heart in a heart that was after God... so, that heart is being born again. He puts a new spirit and a new heart, then he places His Spirit in us that we might hear and obey Him.

Ezekiel 36:24 For I will take you from among the heathen, and gather you out of all countries, and will bring you into your own land. 25 Then will I sprinkle clean water upon you, and ye shall be clean: from all your filthiness, and from all your idols, will I cleanse you. 26 A new heart also will I give you, and a new spirit will I put within you: and I will take away the stony heart out of your flesh, and I will give you an heart of flesh. 27 And I will put my spirit within you, and cause you to walk in my statutes, and ye shall keep my judgments, and do [them]. 28 And ye shall dwell in the land that I gave to your fathers; and ye shall be my people, and I will be your

God. 29 I will also save you from all your uncleannesses: and I will call for the corn, and will increase it, and lay no famine upon you. 30 And I will multiply the fruit of the tree, and the increase of the field, that ye shall receive no more reproach of famine among the heathen. 31 Then shall ye remember your own evil ways, and your doings that [were] not good, and shall lothe yourselves in your own sight for your iniquities and for your abominations.

2 Corinthians 5:17 Therefore if any man [be] in Christ, [he is] a new creature: old things are passed away; behold, all things are become new.

HOW does Salvation start?

It is up to us repent of our sins and to accept His Ultimate Sacrifice. Now He will help us live the rest of our lives for Him.

Romans 10:9 That if thou shalt confess with thy mouth the Lord Jesus, and shalt believe in thine heart that God hath raised him from the dead, thou shalt be saved.

Ephesians 2:8 For by grace are ye saved through faith; and that not of yourselves: [it is] the gift of God: 9 Not of works, lest any man should boast. 10 For we are his workmanship, created in Christ Jesus unto good works, which God hath before ordained that we should walk in them.

John 3:15 That whosoever believeth in him should not perish, but have eternal life. 16 For God so loved the world that he gave his only begotten Son, that whosoever believeth in him should not perish, but have everlasting life. 17 For God sent not his Son into the world to condemn the world; but that the world through him might be saved. 18 He that believeth on him is not condemned: but he that believeth not is condemned already, because he hath not believed in the name of the only begotten Son of God. 19 And this is the condemnation, that light is come into the world, and men loved darkness rather than light, because their deeds were evil. 20 For every one that doeth evil hateth the light, neither cometh to the light, lest his deeds should be reproved. 21 But he that doeth truth cometh to the light, that his deeds may be made manifest, that they are wrought in God.

WHY is it a process?

After we have accepted His Salvation we must allow God guide us in this new life 39

Philippians 2:12 Wherefore, my beloved, as ye have always obeyed, not as in my presence only, but now much more in my absence, work out your own salvation with fear and trembling. 13 For it is God which worketh in you both to will and to do of [his] good pleasure.

Isaiah 26:12 LORD, thou wilt ordain peace for us: for thou also hast wrought all our works in us. 13 O LORD our God, [other] lords beside thee have had dominion over us: [but] by thee only will we make mention of thy name. 14 [They are] dead, they shall not live; [they are] deceased, they shall not rise: therefore hast thou visited and destroyed them, and made all their memory to perish.

HOW can we protect such a great gift?

- Walk in the Light

1 John 1:4 And these things write we unto you, that your joy may be full. 5 This then is the message which we have heard of him, and declare unto you, that God is light, and in him is no darkness at all. 6 If we say that we have fellowship with him, and walk in darkness, we lie, and do not the truth:

- Have Fellowship with God and Other Saints

7 But if we walk in the light, as he is in the light, we have fellowship one with another, and the blood of Jesus Christ his Son cleanseth us from all sin.

- Keep our Sins Confessed

8 If we say that we have no sin, we deceive ourselves, and the truth is not in us. 9 If we confess our sins, he is faithful and just to forgive us [our] sins, and to cleanse us from all unrighteousness. 10 If we say that we have not sinned, we make him a liar, and his word is not in us.
John 3: 21 But he that doeth truth cometh to the light, that his deeds may be made manifest, that they are wrought in God.

CAN YOU lose Salvation?

Hebrews 6:1 Therefore leaving the principles of the doctrine of Christ, let us go on unto perfection; not laying again the foundation of repentance from dead works, and of faith toward God, 2 Of the doctrine of baptisms, and of laying on of hands, and of resurrection of the dead, and of eternal judgment. 3 And this will we do, if God permit. 4 For [it is] impossible for those who were once enlightened, and have tasted of the heavenly gift, and were made partakers of the Holy Ghost, 5 And have tasted the good word of God, and the powers of the world to come, 6 If they shall fall away, to renew them again unto repentance; seeing they crucify to themselves the Son of God afresh, and put [him] to an open shame.

REVIEW: WHAT IS SALVATION?

1. Salvation is the gift that comes through _____ Jesus, the ultimate sacrifice.

2. We need salvation because Adam's _____ _____ him and all his _____ from God

3. What happen during salvation? When Jesus died on the cross He took _____ into the grave. He went right into _____ and took the _____ that _____ us from God away from Satan and Jesus won the battle right there. for you and I. Salvation starts now it's up to us to _____it!

4. Therefore, if any man be _____ _____, he is a _____ _____: old things are _____ _____; behold, all things are become _____.

5. Salvation - "That if thou shalt _____ with thy mouth the

_____ _____, and shalt believe in thine _____ that God hath _____ him from the dead, thou shalt be _____."

6. But he that doeth _____ cometh to the _____, that his deeds may be made manifest, that they are wrought in God.

7. Process - After we have accepted His _____ we must _____ God to _____ us in this new life.

8. Protect the Gift (of Salvation) - Have Fellowship: But if we _____ in the light, as he is in the light, we have fellowship one with another, and the _____ of Jesus Christ his Son cleanseth us from all sin. Keep our sin _____.

9. Can You Lose Your Salvation? - "And have tasted the good word of God, and the powers of the world to come, if they shall _____ _____, to renew them again unto _____; seeing they crucify to themselves the Son of God _____, and put him to an open _____."

8
WHAT IS WATER BAPTISM?

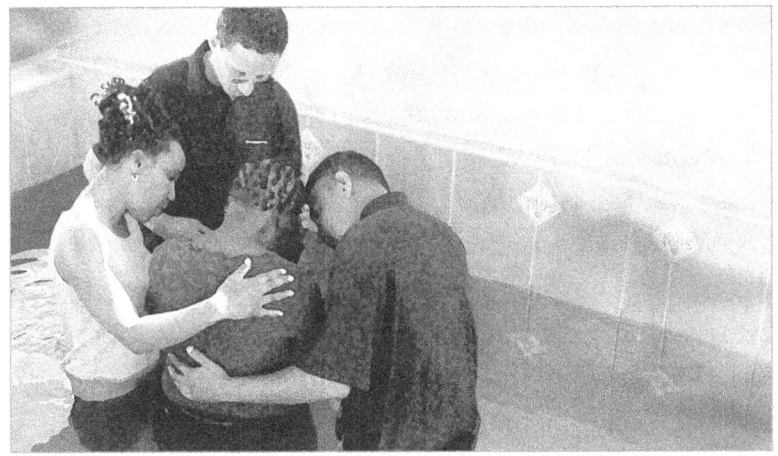

Excerpt "The Power of Water Baptism" by Rev. Agnes I. Numer

"If we would truly understand God's plan for Water Baptism, then when we are baptized in water a lot of our "junk" would be taken care of. Water Baptism is being buried. We are being buried with Jesus. This is powerful, the will to sin, those carnal things in our lives, let's bury them with Him and come up not in any Sin, but in Righteousness.

When Jesus died on the cross He went down into that grave taking the SIN of the whole world upon Him, He went into hell and He took those keys and He snatched them away from Satan and He said now I'm going to give these keys to these that I have redeemed – Jesus won the battle right there for you and I.

This is why it is important for us to be water baptized. It is a part of our Spiritual Foundation.

Through water baptism Jesus says to Satan, "**No longer** will you have control over them. When they go down into that watery grave with Me, **everything** that you have in them is gone. I'll set them free, I'll bring them up in newness of life, I'll bring them up in My resurrection power. You have no more dominion over them Satan, I've taken it away from you and I've placed it in their hands. And now they have power and dominion over you."

What are we teaching? What has been given to man? Satan has no more dominion over you when you go down into that water, you lay that old carnal self, down into that water. You just give that carnal self back to Satan and tell him to take it back to the pit. Now, you come forth out of Water Baptism in the mighty resurrection power of Jesus Christ.

You are going to come forth; you died there and left that carnal world behind. As Jesus brought you up He brought you up into Resurrection Life, He placed in your hands the keys to the Kingdom, the keys over Satan. Hear me... And He brought you forth set free, made free from sin through His precious blood and death. Even as He took the keys from Satan, as you come forth in Him in resurrection power – you now have the keys in your hand!

This is the word of God; this is the power of the Gospel, of the Kingdom of God, and this same Spirit that raised Jesus from the dead quickens your mortal body.

You come up out of that water with newness of life, you come out a new creature, and you come out a Son of God. It is not the water... but it's what Jesus said to do and then He would set us free. But if we don't know the truth, how are we going to enter into it? This is one of the most valuable lessons for us to enter into the power and authority of Jesus Christ.

This is where grace begins...

Through Water Baptism, sin is left in the watery grave, and grace begins, and how great is that grace."

The word godly means, reflecting the attributes or nature of God. But water baptism is not just us reflecting God's attributes. It is His nature, inside of us. When we are baptized, God speaks into our spirit, just like he spoke over Jesus "This is My beloved Son." He speaks into us His nature. Just as if we had never sinned. This new nature loves what God loves.

This is the beginning of a process.

Study the statements and questions below and allow God to reveal the power of Water Baptism to you.

WHO was John the Baptist?

Water Baptism was first performed in the Bible by John the Baptist. John came to prepare men's hearts by preaching repentance and baptism. This was new for the Jews they only made sacrifices and washings.

Isaiah 40:3 The voice of him that crieth in the wilderness, Prepare ye the way of the LORD, make straight in the desert a highway for our God.

Mark 1:1 The beginning of the gospel of Jesus Christ, the Son of God; 2 As it is written in the prophets, Behold, I send my messenger before thy face, which shall prepare thy way before thee. 3 The voice of one crying in the wilderness, Prepare ye the way of the Lord, make his paths straight. 4 John did baptize in the wilderness, and preach the baptism of repentance for the remission of sins. 5 And there went out unto him all the land of Judaea, and they of Jerusalem, and were all baptized of him in the river of Jordan, confessing their sins.

John the Baptist said a believer must produce fruits that show true repentance. Examples include: benevolence, kindness, love, generosity, honesty, justice, faithfulness, meekness, quietness, temperance and contentment.

Luke 3:8 Bring forth therefore fruits worthy of repentance, and begin not to say within yourselves, We have Abraham to [our] father: for I say unto you, That God is able of these stones to raise up children unto Abraham.

John the Baptist prophesied that the Messiah was coming and that He would "baptize with the Holy Spirit and fire".

Luke 3:16 John answered, saying unto [them] all, I indeed baptize you with water; but one mightier than I cometh, the latchet of whose shoes I am not worthy to unloose: he shall baptize you with the Holy Ghost and with fire:

Examples of Baptism in the Old Testament

1 Corinthians 10:1 Moreover, brethren, I would not that ye should be ignorant, how that all our fathers were under the cloud, and all passed through the sea;

2 And were all baptized unto Moses in the cloud and in the sea;

WHY did Jesus choose to be Water Baptized?

Jesus came to the River Jordan to be baptized of John the Baptist. When John tried to prevent Him Jesus asked for John to "permit it at this time" in order to "fulfill all righteousness" Jesus obeyed God in Water Baptism to show us an example. The Holy Spirit descended on Jesus after He was baptized.

Matthew 3:13 Then cometh Jesus from Galilee to Jordan unto John, to be baptized of him. 14 But John forbad him, saying, I have need to be baptized of thee, and comest thou to me? 15 And Jesus answering said unto him, Suffer [it to be so] now: for thus it becometh us to fulfil all righteousness. Then he suffered him. 16 And Jesus, when he was baptized, went up straightway out of the water: and, lo, the heavens were opened unto him, and he saw the Spirit of God descending like a dove, and lighting upon him: 17 And lo a voice from heaven, saying, This is my beloved Son, in whom I am well pleased.

1 Peter 2:21 For even hereunto were ye called: because Christ also suffered for us, leaving us an example, that ye should follow his steps:

God gave John a sign that Jesus was Christ the Messiah;

and that he would see the Holy Spirit "descending and remaining upon him."

John 1:29 The next day John seeth Jesus coming unto him, and saith, Behold the Lamb of God, which taketh away the sin of the world. 4:30 This is he of whom I said, After me cometh a man which is preferred before me: for he was before me. 31 And I knew him not: but that he should be made manifest to Israel, therefore am I come baptizing with water. 32 And John bare record, saying, I saw the Spirit descending from heaven like a dove, and it abode upon him. 33 And I knew him not: but he that sent me to baptize with water, the same said unto me, Upon whom thou shalt see the Spirit descending, and remaining on him, the same is he which baptizeth with the Holy Ghost.

WHAT is Water Baptism?

Water Baptism is when a believer in Jesus allows himself to be immersed under water symbolizing the Death and Resurrection of Jesus Christ.

Acts 8:36 And as they went on [their] way, they came unto a certain water: and the eunuch said, See, [here is] water; what doth hinder me to be baptized? 37 And Philip said, If thou believest with all thine heart, thou mayest. And he answered and said, I believe that Jesus Christ is the Son of God. 38 And he commanded the chariot to stand still: and they went down both into the water, both Philip and the eunuch; and he baptized him.

Joining Jesus in burial through Water Baptism:

- Destroys the DNA – (the sin nature) of Adam
- Replaces the DNA – (the New nature) of Jesus Christ.

Through Water Baptism we trade the sin nature of Adam with the New God breathed nature of Jesus Christ!

We are no longer slaves to sin, but of love, we are servants of righteousness

Through Water Baptism the Holy Spirit empowers us to live a life of freedom from being bound to sin.

We must not let sin rule and reign in our bodies. We are free to live in righteousness unto God. We are no longer slaves to sin, but of love, we are servants of righteousness.

Romans 6:3 Know ye not, that so many of us as were baptized into Jesus Christ were baptized into his death? 4 Therefore we are buried with him by baptism into death: that like as Christ was raised up from the dead by the glory of the Father, even so we also should walk in newness of life.

Rom 6:18 Being then made free from sin, ye became the servants of righteousness.

WHO Should be Water Baptized?

Water Baptism – a Statement to the World!

Notice that everyone was baptized. This is the mark of a

follower of Christ. It is a statement for all to see. In many cultures, once you have been baptized a Christian you could be excommunicated or killed. You are saying, "I have decided to follow Jesus... No turning back"

1 Corinthians 12:13 For by one Spirit are we all baptized into one body, whether [we be] Jews or Gentiles, whether [we be] bond or free; and have been all made to drink into one Spirit.

Mark 16:16 He that believeth and is baptized shall be saved; but he that believeth not shall be damned.

Acts 2:38 Then Peter said unto them, Repent, and be baptized every one of you in the name of Jesus Christ for the remission of sins, and ye shall receive the gift of the Holy Ghost.

JESUS instructs us to baptize all nations.

Matt 28:18 And Jesus came and spake unto them, saying, All power is given unto me in heaven and in earth. 19 Go ye therefore, and teach all nations, baptizing them in the name of the Father, and of the Son, and of the Holy Ghost: 20 Teaching them to observe all things whatsoever I have commanded you: and, lo, I am with you alway, [even] unto the end of the world.

Excerpt from "Allowing God's Perfect Peace" by Rev. Agnes I. Numer

Jesus Destroyed The "Old Man Of Sin"

"You know, I was trained in a church that talked about sanctification. Then when I started reading the Word the way God gave it to me, I saw something different. They're talking about the old man of sin. Did you ever meet him? Did you ever know him? He's got a lot of Christians bewildered. Do you know what that means? I use to think that, well, it's your carnality that's showing. This use to be an expression in a church I was raised in. If you raised your voice or you said something that they didn't approve of, "Oh, that's your carnality showing!" I got news for you. Jesus said He took it to the cross. He forgave our sins through His shed blood. He destroyed Adam's sin in you, so what did He do? He took it to the cross. It was a curse placed there by the fall of man.

Jesus took it to the cross. When we are baptized in water, we have the privilege of carrying "the old man" down there and burying him. He'll let us carry that old man of sin... but He destroyed him on the cross, destroyed his power on the cross ...for every Christian, that will hear it and obey it. You go down into that water, a grave with the Lord, and you bury that old man there. He isn't alive when you go down. He's already dead, he died at the cross. **But you have the privilege of burying him**, so you know for sure he's not alive.

What a relief it was for me when God opened that scripture because I thought that all my life I was going to have to put up with that old man of sin and walk with Jesus. Thank God it isn't true! We might have a lot of things we need to get rid of, but we have Jesus and He'll get rid of it for us. Amen!

He said it is so very important for us to be baptized in water, into Jesus Christ. Not into a church, not the Methodist church, not into the Baptist church, not into the

Catholic Church, but into Jesus Christ. John's baptism was a baptism of repentance, but the baptism of Jesus is to bring us into Him. And He into us – making us into a quickened spirit. **No longer of Adam's race, but a new creature** – a new creation formed right there by Jesus Christ, as we go down to the cross and as we go down into the water. The old man is buried there, never to rise again, as long as we allow Jesus Christ to be the Lord and King in His kingdom in our life.

If we forsake Him, then we are going to go through hell. You're going to go through the horrible things that Satan has for you. But if you hold fast to the Lord and you do what He says, this mighty work that He has given us is complete in Jesus Christ. "In Him we live, we move, we have our being." **He's the one who gives us perfect peace, and it stays with us.** He ordained it for us. He made it possible for us. He made it possible for us to be baptized in water, as well, that we might be free from the old man of sin and that we might live in His peace to destroy all the affects of this life."

God has given us the answer.

REVIEW: WHAT IS WATER BAPTISM?

1. _____ _____ is when a believer in Jesus allows himself to be immersed under water symbolizing the Death and Resurrection of Jesus Christ.
a. confessing sins
b. water baptism
c. sinner's prayer
d. new believer

2. Water baptism _____ the DNA – (the _____ nature) of Adam and _____ it with the DNA (the _____ nature) of Jesus Christ.

3. We are no longer of Adam's race, but a new creature – a new creation formed right there by Jesus Christ.

4. Through Water Baptism we _____ the _____ nature of Adam with the _____ nature of Jesus Christ!

5. Through Water Baptism the Holy Spirit empowers us to live a life of freedom from being bound to sin.

6. Who Should be Water Baptized?
a. only church members
b. those who have finished the new believer's class
c. anyone who believes that Jesus is the son of God and died for our sins
d. Only Gentile believers

9

WHO IS THE HOLY SPIRIT?

God is one God. You have heard of God the Father, God the Son and God the Holy Spirit – this is one God. Three in One. Water, ice and steam are different forms of water – they are all still water – but different forms; with God He is all three at the same time.

This is something we don't easily understand because

we can only be in one place at one time. But think about this, we are a spirit, who lives in a body and has a soul. That makes us in the image of God. When we die our body is buried, yet our spirit lives on forever.

Study the statements and questions below and **allow God to reveal Himself to you.**

WHO is the Holy Spirit?

Holy Spirit is God. He is a person. The Holy Spirit is the one who helps us realize our sin. He does not have a physical body because He is a Spirit. Sometimes people call Him the Holy Ghost. This is just a different word which means the Holy Spirit. God's nature is love and since the Holy Spirit is God He is love also.

The Holy Spirit's work is on the Earth. He works in the hearts of people. He can speak to us in our hearts; we can hear Him or sense Him with our spirit. He also helps us to feel when we have sinned. The Holy Spirit was there when God created the world.

Genesis 1:26 And God said, Let us make man in our image, after our likeness:...

The Old Testament is the first part of the Bible written before Jesus was born. The New Testament was written after Jesus was born. The Old Testament books were written by men who were "moved" by the Holy Spirit.

2 Peter 1:21 For the prophecy came not in old time by the will of man: but holy men of God spake as they were moved by the Holy Ghost.

The Holy Spirit can also "move" our hearts to do things, which means He gives us special abilities that come from God at certain times to do what God wants.

Here are examples from the Old Testament of abilities that God gave by the Holy Spirit. Wisdom - Solomon, I Kings 4:29-32, Knowledge - Elisha, II Kings 5:25-27, Discerning of Spirits - Saul's Servant, - I Samuel 16:14-15, Faith - Joshua, Joshua 10:12-14, Miracles - Elijah I Kings 17:17-24, I Kings 18:38, Healings - Isaiah II Kings 20:5, Prophecy - Balaam Numbers 23:24,

We may ask the Holy Spirit for **special abilities** whenever we need them to do what God wants. He is here for the purpose of helping God's people to do God's will on Earth.

WHO is the Holy Spirit to Us?

The Holy Spirit is:

Our Teacher. He leads us and guides us into the Truth. He will "steer us" away from lies and deception. Have you ever played the game where you pick an object in the room and lead someone to it by just using the words "hotter" or "colder"? We will begin to learn that "nudge" in our hearts. We will learn to "hear His voice" We can trust Him to teach us.

Our Comforter. He will be with us always, in every circumstance, in every trouble or joy. He wants us to feel His presence with us. We just need to ask. We can trust Him to comfort us.

Our Helper. He helps us pray even when we don't know what to say. He will help us in so many ways. He will give us special spiritual abilities that come from God. We can trust Him to help us to live God's way.

1 Corinthians 12:1 Now concerning spiritual gifts, brethren, I would not have you ignorant....... 7 But the manifestation of the Spirit is given to every man to profit withal. 8 For to one is given by the Spirit the word of wisdom; to another the word of knowledge by the same Spirit; 9 To another faith by the same Spirit; to another the gifts of healing by the same Spirit; 10 To another the working of miracles; to another prophecy; to another discerning of spirits; to another divers kinds of tongues; to another the interpretation of tongues: 11 But all these worketh that one and the selfsame Spirit, dividing to every man severally as he will.

WE CAN TRUST the Holy Spirit, we just need to ask.

REVIEW: WHO IS THE HOLY SPIRIT?

1. Our God is:
a. Three in one
b. Father, Son and Holy Spirit
c. One God
d. All of the above

2. How are we made in God's image?
a. Spirit, Soul and body
b. Water, ice and steam
c. Able to be everywhere at once
d. We always existed

3. The Holy Spirit:
a. Is God
b. Does not have a physical body
c. All of the above
d. None of the above

4. The Old Testament was written by men moved by the Holy Spirit.
a. True
b. False

5. The Holy Spirit can give special God given abilities to man like:
a. Knowledge
b. Prophesy
c. Miracles
d. All of the Above

6. The Holy Spirit is here for the purpose of helping God's people to do God's will on Earth
a. True
b. False

7. As our teacher, the Holy Spirit guides us into the Truth.
a. True
b. False

8. The Holy Spirit can help us pray even when we don't know what to say.
a. True
b. False

10
WHAT IS THE BAPTISM OF THE HOLY SPIRIT?

S tudy the statements and questions below and allow the Holy Spirit to reveal Himself to you.

What is the Baptism of the Holy Spirit?

The plan of God to bring people back to Himself was paid for by Jesus coming and dying in our place on a cross. This opened the way for people to be made clean from sin. The Old Testament sacrifices only covered our past sins and they had to be repeated every year; but Jesus came to restore people back to Father God. We now can come to Him at any time through Jesus.

God has eagerly waited to walk with us again and talk with us and give us His special abilities we had lost. The way was open for this through Jesus. Jesus had to return to His Father after He died and resurrected again so that He could send us the Holy Spirit. He knew how much we needed His Spirit to be living IN US and not just WITH US.

John 14:17 Even the Spirit of truth; whom the world cannot receive, because it seeth him not, neither knoweth him: but ye know him; for he dwelleth with you, and shall be in you.

Something more was promised to us

The Holy Spirit already convicts us of our sin, applies the blood of Jesus, draws us to Jesus, and leads us and guides us; but there is more! Father God promised more, Jesus talked about it and even John the Baptist said there was MORE.

John the Baptist said that Jesus would baptize us with the Holy Spirit and fire. Fire cleans and purifies, gives light and heat (zeal and boldness). Luke 3:16 - He will baptize you with the Holy Spirit and with fire.

Matt 3:11 I indeed baptize you with water unto repentance: but he that cometh after me is mightier than I, whose shoes I am not worthy to bear: he shall baptize you with the Holy Ghost, and with fire:

How did Jesus describe the coming of the Holy Spirit?

We would **receive power.**

Acts 1:8 But ye shall receive power, after that the Holy Ghost is come upon you: and ye shall be witnesses unto me both in Jerusalem, and in all Judaea, and in Samaria, and unto the uttermost part of the earth.

We would have **rivers of living water** flowing out of us.

John 7:38 He that believeth on me, as the scripture hath said, out of his belly shall flow rivers of living water. 39 (But this spake he of the Spirit, which they that believe on him should receive: for the Holy Ghost was not yet given; because that Jesus was not yet glorified.)

This is what **my Father has promised** you. Luke 24:49 - Behold I sent the promise of My Father upon you.

Acts 1:4 - He commanded them not to depart from Jerusalem, but to wait for the Promise of the Father.

Luke 11:13 - How much more will your heavenly Father give the Holy Spirit to those that ask Him?

Acts 2:39 - For the promise is to you, and to your children, and to all who are afar off, as many as the Lord our God will call.

They were told they must wait for the Holy Spirit

We cannot do what God wants on our own. We need to be filled with His power. This is why Jesus insisted that they wait together until they receive power when the Holy Spirit came... then they could be his witnesses. Acts 1:4

What Did They Experience?

There was something very life changing that happened to the people who followed Jesus after he returned to heaven. After waiting 50 days, on the days the Jews call Pentecost they experienced everything Jesus had promised to them. They received The Baptism of the Holy Spirit and fire.

> Acts 2:1 And when the day of Pentecost was fully come, they were all with one accord in one place. 2 And suddenly there came a sound from heaven as of a rushing mighty wind, and it filled all the house where they were sitting. 3 And there appeared unto them cloven tongues like as of fire, and it sat upon each of them. 4 And they were all filled with the Holy Ghost, and began to speak with other tongues, as the Spirit gave them utterance. 5 And there were dwelling at Jerusalem Jews, devout men, out of every nation under heaven. 6 Now when this was noised abroad, the multitude came together, and were confounded, because that every man heard them speak in his own language. 7 And they were all amazed and marvelled, saying one to another, Behold, are not all these which speak Galilaeans? 8 And how hear we every man in our own tongue, wherein we were born? 9 Parthians, and Medes, and Elamites, and the dwellers in Mesopotamia, and in Judaea, and Cappadocia, in Pontus, and Asia, 10 Phrygia, and Pamphylia, in Egypt, and in the parts of Libya about Cyrene, and strangers of Rome, Jews and proselytes, 11 Cretes and Arabians, we do hear them speak in our tongues the wonderful works of God. 12 And they were all amazed, and were in doubt, saying one to another, What

meaneth this? 13 Others mocking said, These men are full of new wine.14 But Peter, standing up with the eleven, lifted up his voice, and said unto them, Ye men of Judaea, and all ye that dwell at Jerusalem, be this known unto you, and hearken to my words:

Acts 2:15 For these are not drunken, as ye suppose, seeing it is but the third hour of the day. 16 But this is that which was spoken by the prophet Joel; 17 And it shall come to pass in the last days, saith God, I will pour out of my Spirit upon all flesh: and your sons and your daughters shall prophesy, and your young men shall see visions, and your old men shall dream dreams: 18 And on my servants and on my handmaidens I will pour out in those days of my Spirit; and they shall prophesy: 19 And I will shew wonders in heaven above, and signs in the earth beneath; blood, and fire, and vapour of smoke: 20 The sun shall be turned into darkness, and the moon into blood, before that great and notable day of the Lord come.

What Acts Did the Baptism of the Holy Spirit Cause?

Boldness

The same man, Peter, who had been too afraid to admit to a slave girl that he was a follower of Jesus was filled with such boldness that he stood up in front of thousands of people and declared Jesus to be the Son of God and all men should repent and turn to God.

A Message from God

The Holy Spirit gave a special ability to be able to speak God's words to the people

Conviction

This is when the Holy Spirit is working in a person's heart and helping him to realize and be sorry for his sins. As the message was being spoken people's hearts were moved

Repentance

Thousands of people admitted their sins and their need of God because the Holy Spirit was convincing their hearts and leading them to repent.

Speaking In Tongues

All of the people who became baptized in the Holy Spirit were speaking in different languages as the Holy Spirit gave them words. Some of them spoke in languages which they had never learned, but people from other countries who heard it could understand. This sign convinced many people that God was at work.

Miracles

The Holy Spirit gave the apostles special ability to do many miracles that further convinced people that what was happening came from God.

Acts 2:43 And fear came upon every soul: and many wonders and signs were done by the apostles.

This promise is for us today.

Peter said this promise was for them, for their children and for those who would live many generations from then. It was for all people for all time. This is what the Father has desired for so long.... To restore to us what we lost because of sin and to become his people filled with His Spirit, with the same power as they experienced in Acts 2

Acts 2:39 For the promise is unto you, and to your children, and to all that are afar off, even as many as the Lord our God shall call.

Who can receive the Baptism of the Holy Spirit?

Whoever will repent and be baptized

> 38 Then Peter said unto them, Repent, and be baptized every one of you in the name of Jesus Christ for the remission of sins, and ye shall receive the gift of the Holy Ghost.

Whoever will ask Father God for the Holy Spirit

> Luke 11:13 - How much more will your heavenly Father give the Holy Spirit to those that ask Him?

Whoever will receive the gift

> Repent, and be baptized every one of you in the name of Jesus Christ for the remission of sins, and ye shall receive the gift of the Holy Ghost.

Our Heavenly Father God has made such a wonderful plan to bring us back to what He desired to give to Adam and Eve. He wants to place His Holy Spirit IN US so we can be filled with power and fire and the Holy Spirit can continue HIS ACTS through us. Please ask Him for that gift today.

REVIEW: WHAT IS THE BAPTISM OF THE HOLY SPIRIT?

1. Jesus opened the way for us to:
a. Live forever
b. Again, receive God's special abilities through the Holy Spirit
c. Live a life full of pleasure and wealth
d. Become powerful spiritual beings on Earth

2. What did Jesus say we would receive when the Holy Spirit comes upon us?
a. Power
b. Rivers of Living Water
c. The ability to be witnesses to the World
d. All of the Above

3. We are able to become witnesses to the world without the Holy Spirit's help.
a. True
b. False

4. When did Jesus followers receive the promise?
a. After 50 days
b. When they were all in unity in one place
c. After Jesus returned to heaven
d. All of the above

5. What caused the boldness, miracles and powerful messages in the lives of Jesus followers?
a. They were drunk with wine
b. They had been with Jesus for 3 years already
c. They received the gift of the Holy Spirit
d. None of the above

6. This gift was only for the original followers of Jesus so they would have a strong start.
a. True
b. False

7. Who is qualified to receive the promised gift of the Holy Spirit?
a. Whoever will repent and be baptized
b. Whoever asks the Father
c. Whoever desires to receive this gift
d. All of the above

11

WHAT MUST I DO TO BE SAVED?

How do I know I am going to heaven?

Realize that you need to be saved, God is in heaven and sin separates us from God forever. God does not want us to be separated from Him, so God gave His only

Son Jesus, to pay the price of our sins by dying on a cross many years ago.

Romans 3:23 For all have sinned, and come short of the glory of God;

Romans 6:23 For the wages of sin is death, but the gift of God is eternal life through Jesus Christ our Lord.

Romans 5:8 But God commendeth his love toward us, in that, while we were yet sinners, Christ died for us.

We must believe on Jesus and cry out to the God who created us in the beginning and ask Him for a personal relationship with Him as our Father, Creator and Lord.

Ezekiel 36:24 For I will take you from among the heathen, and gather you out of all countries, and will bring you into your own land. 25 Then will I sprinkle clean water upon you, and ye shall be clean: from all your filthiness, and from all your idols, will I cleanse you. 26 A new heart also will I give you, and a new spirit will I put within you: and I will take away the stony heart out of your flesh, and I will give you an heart of flesh. 27 And I will put my spirit within you, and cause you to walk in my statutes, and ye shall keep my judgments, and do them.

John 3:15 That whosoever believeth in him should not perish, but have eternal life. 16 For God so loved the world, that he gave his only begotten Son, that whosoever believeth in him should not perish, but have everlasting life. 17 For God sent not his Son into the world to condemn the world; but that the world through him might be saved. 18 He that believeth on him is not condemned: but he that believeth not is condemned already, because he hath not believed in the name of the only begotten Son of God. 19 And this is the condemnation, that light is come into the world, and men loved darkness rather than light, because their deeds were evil. 20 For every one that doeth evil hateth the light, neither cometh to the light, lest his deeds should be reproved. 21 But he that doeth truth cometh to the light, that his deeds may be made manifest, that they are wrought in God.

Pray this prayer with us:

Dear Jesus, I know that I have sinned I have chosen to do things that are wrong when I could have chosen the right. I repent from those sins; I want and need for my life to change... Today. Please forgive me and place your new heart and your new spirit with in me. Please come and live in my heart forever. Jesus, please guide me in your ways and cause me to please you and not this world. Fill my heart with your love and compassion for others and guide me all of the days of my life. Amen.

Now, look for a church that believes in the Bible as the Word of God. Find out what the next steps are to being a Christian, following this beautiful Jesus and knowing God as your Father and being led by His Spirit. God bless you.

12

GO MAKE DISCIPLES

What is a disciple?
    Definition: A follower or student of a teacher, belief or philosophy. Synonyms: Follower, adherent, believer, student, pupil, devotee… **Follow Me.**

When Jesus called his disciples he simply said, "Follow me and **I will make you** fishers of men" Matthew 4:19

He did not say, "Follow your heart, Trust your instincts, or Do what is in your heart". Not even "follow your dreams". These are all modern, common clichés which make our dreams and ideas the things to follow. Every man doing what is right in his own eyes.

Jesus said, "Take up your cross and follow me.." He said, "**learn** of me for my yoke is easy and my burden is light".

Before the invention of encyclopedias and later the internet, search engines and the cloud where you can find information to learn almost anything you want; knowledge was passed mostly from person to person by word of mouth and life example. There were "Masters", and teachers; Lords who you could follow. If they saw you had potential to be a good disciple/follower who would carry their **way** to others and to the next generation they would allow you to learn from them. This is how they spread ideologies and lifestyles. In some countries there is still the concept of an apprentice who studies and works under a Master Craftsman. There are still gurus (spiritual masters) who will lead disciples into their spiritual way such as Hare Krishna. There are those who follow Mohamed's teachings of Islam and are called Muslims.

All or Nothing

Jesus also said, "...anyone who does not give up everything he has cannot be My disciple" Luke 14:33. He was saying we must give up our own pursuits in order to pursue Him. Seek first His Kingdom.

Hands on training

Jesus was calling His disciples to follow Him and learn

His ways which came from His Father. They spent over three years with Him going everywhere He went and doing everything He did. These 12 main followers ate together, journeyed together and slept together. They saw Jesus pray, they heard Him teach, they saw Him cry, and they saw Him laugh. He instructed them and corrected them. He taught them to do what He did, to heal every manner of sickness, cast out devils and preach about the Kingdom of Heaven.

Jesus sent out His disciples to do as He did

One day, after they had been with Jesus for some time He sent them out to begin proclaiming the same message they had learned from Him. They went healing the sick, casting out demons and simply trusting God for Him to provide everything they needed as they went. The same miracles that Jesus did they did. They preached the same message with the same results. The disciples were so excited that people were healed and even the devils were subject to them. Jesus told them that what they needed to be happy about was that their names were written in the book of life.

Jesus commissioned His disciples before He left to reach the whole world with this message.

When Jesus knew He was soon to be crucified, He commissioned His followers; He told them to go out and make disciples in all of the surrounding nations. He told His followers to teach them everything He had taught to them.

Jesus told them that their disciples would do the same miracles and teach the same message.

He said that they who believed their word would also heal the sick, raise the dead and cast out devils. They would not be afraid of deadly things because they would not be harmed. Mark 16:16-17 Jesus had given His authority to

His disciples to preach, heal and deliver; but then He commissioned those disciples to "train" others to do the same things.

He called them His disciples, He called them His friends and then He called them His brothers.

The wonderful truth is that not only are we called to be followers but we are called to be sons of God. A part of the family. Jesus is our brother. We are adopted in by our Father God because Jesus opened the way.

"You are my friends if you do the things I tell you" John 15:14

Paul, who never actually met Jesus said, "Follow me as I follow Christ"

Read 1 Corinthians 3:6-21. Here, Paul urges the people not to follow human leaders like the world does. The human leaders are given by God to direct people to Father God. Then Paul urges us, "As a Christian, do not be proud of men and of what they can do. All things belong to you." (1 Corinthians 3:21 NLV) Paul also warns the human leaders to be careful what they build onto the foundation which is Christ Jesus. Paul then says in verse 23 "You belong to Christ, and Christ belongs to God.".

Paul writes that this is how you should look at human Christian leaders:

- They are servants of Christ
- They have been given insight into God's Truth
- They are stewards of the Mysteries God has given them to give to others
- They are required to be faithful to serve the followers of Christ (see 1 Corinthians 4:2)

- God knows the motives of their hearts (see 1 Corinthians 4:5)
- They will be judged by their inner motivations. (also 1 Corinthians 4:5)
- They should be more like Fathers not merely Teachers. "You may have 10,000 Christian teachers. But remember, I am the only father you have. You became Christians when I preached the Good News to you." 1 Corinthians 4:15 (NLV)
- Their lives should match their teachings everywhere they go. See 1 Corinthians 4:17.

The Old Testament

Being a follower of God did not just begin in the New Testament. The books of the Old Testament records the stories of people who were both good and poor examples to us.

God said these very sad words about King Saul, "He has turned away from **following after** Me." 1 Samuel 15:10-11. God said essentially, "because he has turned away from following me I have rejected him as king and I am sorry I ever made him ruler of my people". On his own no man has the right to lead His sheep, **they are His** and He is the Good Shepherd. **We cannot lead unless we are personally following, hearing and obeying.**

While Moses was leading the people through the wilderness they had the arc of the covenant, a symbol of His presence, in the center of the camp. There was a cloud of His presence above during the day and a pillar of fire during the night. When it was time for them to move to a new place the cloud would lift up and they would all prepare to move. They followed the cloud. This was their **protection and direction.** This is a type of Spirit lead believers today. Other nations feared to attack because of the glory. Today believers must be led by the Spirit of God Romans 8:14

An example of someone who followed, trusted and pleased God was Caleb. He was a man who lived his life pursuing and believing the promises of God even though most of the people around him allowed themselves to doubt, grumble and disobey. Numbers 32:11

"But my servant Caleb, because he **has a different spirit and has followed me fully**, I will bring into the land into which he went, (as a spy) and his descendants **shall possess it.**" Numbers 14:24

The man Enoch walked with God and he talked with God. He knew Him and loved Him then one day "he was not for God took him". Genesis 5:22-24

How can you follow a God you cannot see?

We follow the Holy Scriptures. There are very clear commands and instructions in the Bible to guide and direct our lives into what is right.

We follow the leading and teaching of the Holy Spirit as He gives us personal and specific direction if we are sensitive to Him.

We follow the teaching of our spiritual leaders who God has placed in our life for our good.

We follow those who have gone before us. We can take examples from people God has used powerfully. We can read their books and come to understand many things about how God worked with them and then apply it to our lives.

Like Enoch, we can walk with God for ourselves. We can know Him and we can hear His voice. We can follow Him all of the days of our lives. We can be His Disciple. We can be His son. We can be His Friend if we obey Him. It is natural for a believer to hear God's voice and be led by the urging and moving of the Holy Spirit who lives within them.

One matter which is very close to the heart of Father God is the souls of those who Jesus died for. He wants us to reach them and make disciples of those who will believe our words.

Go, preach, teach and baptize and make disciples of all nations. Matthew 28:19, Mark 16:15-16

REVIEW: GO MAKE DISCIPLES

1. What is a disciple?
a. A fisher of men
b. A follower or student of a teacher or belief
c. A learned philosopher
d. A teacher of a certain belief or philosophy

2. Which answer best describes a disciple of Jesus?
a. Do what is in your heart
b. Follow your dreams
c. Be the best you that you can be
d. Give up your own pursuits in order to pursue Him

3. Disciples of Jesus are being trained
a. To be good people in this world
b. To do what He is doing in this world
c. To be fishermen
d. To become great leaders in this world

4. Who did Jesus say was supposed to do miracles and teach His message to the world?
a. The 12 apostles only
b. All those who saw him alive and loved His message
c. All those who believed
d. None of the above

5. Paul, who wrote much of the New Testament never actually met Jesus
a. True
b. False

6. Being a follower of God just began in the New Testament.
a. True
b. False

7. We can walk with God ourselves
a. True
b. False

8. We can follow God even though we do not see Him by:
a. Following the scriptures
b. Follow the leading of the Holy Spirit
c. Follow Godly spiritual leaders and those who have lived their lives following God
d. All of the above

REVIEW KEY

Who is God?

1. True
2. a. know, want
3. think, fail, realize, image
4. True
5. b. understand His ways and His commands
6. prepared, showing
7. True
8. Light

Why Did God Make People?

1. c
2. b
3. a

4. d
5. a
6. a

What Is Sin?

1. False
2. sick
3. make, graven, likeness, beneath
4. name, thy, God, guiltless, vain
5. remember, all, do, them, seek, not, own
6. True
7. False
8. True
9. True
10. True
11. c
12. fornication, lasciviousness, hatred, wrath, strife, envyings, drunkenness, do, such, things, inherit
13. created
14. 1 and 2 is how we repent

Who Is Jesus?

1. Son
2. earth
3. man, save
4. ultimate, sin
5. walk, he, fellowship, blood, cleanseth

6. Savior
7. power, sons, believe
8. flesh

What Is Repentance?

1. sinned and come short of the glory
2. d
3. False
4. Sorrow, doing
5. repented
6. pure, see
7. ignoring, you, think, God, right, pray, new, life

What Is Salvation?

1. Accepting
2. sin, separated, descendants
3. sin, hell, keys, separate, receive
4. in, Christ, new, creature, passed, away, new
5. confess, Lord Jesus, believe, heart, raised, saved
6. Truth, light
7. salvation, allow, guide
8. walk, blood, confessed
9. fall away, repentance, afresh, shame

What Is Water Baptism?

1. b. water baptism
2. destroys, sin, replaces, victorious
3. True
4. trade, sin, trade, New
5. True
6. c. anyone who believes that Jesus is the son of God and died for our sins

Who Is the Holy Spirit?

1. d
2. a
3. c
4. True
5. D
6. True
7. True
8. True

What Is the Baptism of the Holy Spirit?

1. a
2. d
3. False
4. b
5. c

6. False
7. d

Go Make Disciples

1. b
2. d
3. b
4. c
5. True
6. False
7. False
8. d

ACKNOWLEDGMENTS

There are so many who are a part of this manual. So many authors and editors, transcribers and artists. It has taken more than 40 years to write this manual.

Thank you to those who have:
1 Corinthians 3:6-8 (NLV)
"I planted the seed. Apollos watered it, but it was God Who kept it growing. This shows that the one who plants or the one who waters is not the important one. God is the important One. He makes it grow. The one who plants and the one who waters are alike. Each one will receive his own reward."

ABOUT THE AUTHOR

For those of you that are wondering... and are interested in... "What are they doing?

Do you remember Rev. Agnes I. Numer sharing about a school? About a college?

Well....

I was with Agnes in the Philippines in the 90's. She sat with maybe 8 men, all of them leaders of Bible Schools and Leadership ministries in the Philippines. When she shared with them that she was going to build a training center in the Philippines, they all said, "Sister Agnes, we are asking you that you would consider having a mobile training team, so that all of our ministries would benefit from your curriculum."

For years we went to different Bible Schools and organizations in the Philippines working with Asian Center for Missions and Tribes and Nations Outreach sharing the principles that God gave to us and through Agnes. Both spiritual and natural teaching like: how to be baptized in the Holy Spirit, how to stay healthy on mission trips, how to raise rabbits and how to flow together and love each other with God's love.

Many of you know, I was so ill for many years. One day, just months before God healed me, He spoke to me and said, "Teresa, you've been doing it wrong. You've been trying to train every person that walked through the door." I was trying to train those who did not want to be trained, those who did not have an ear to hear, a heart to receive, and a heart to obey.

Then God had me read:

2 Timothy 2:2 "And the things that thou hast heard of me among many witnesses, the same commit thou to faithful men, who shall be able to teach others also."

I had cried to the Lord and we had worked with so many and there are so few who took what we learned to the Nations. It seemed unfair to me... how foolish I was. God said, "I trained you... didn't I?" Suddenly I realized how difficult it was to train me... thousands of people later... I definitely repented and was all ears. "Ok, Lord what are you doing?" That was the beginning. The beginning of where we are now.

Shortly before we moved, the Lord told me I would build the school. No, it won't be a school of bricks but a mobile school. No, it won't be for those who will not, it will be for whosoever will... for those who have ears to hear, a heart to receive, a heart to obey. Remember this one?

Habakkuk 2:2 "And the Lord answered me, and said, write the vision, and make it plain upon tables, that he may run that readeth it."

This scripture has resounded inside for many, many years. We started with training paces... but now we must realize it is time. Time to read it and run with it... have you ever thought that in late 7th century BC when the book of Habakkuk was possibly written that there were no iPads or e-readers? This curriculum was made for the modern day "tablet." We have added videos that go right along with the tablet. Now with a couple of wires someone in Africa can use the tablet to have his own Bible School and Training Center.

We are focused on multiplying. We are getting older and time is running away from us. May we spread this truth as far and as fast as God will allow. Empowering Pastors and lay leader the opportunity to teach their people.

What does the curriculum consist of?

Since we have worked with so many Bible Schools our goal will not be to duplicate a regular Bible School with homiletics and hermeneutics... Our goal is:

"What you have heard me say in front of many people, you must teach to faithful men. Then they will be able to teach others also." 2 Timothy 2:2 (NLV)

What God taught us through Agnes and by His Spirit: How to "get the junk out of our lives," how to hear His voice, how to Love the Nations with His Love and how to let Him take us to the Nations.

For others this was "just common stuff." For me it was lifesaving. I would have never made it, I would have never served God and lived through what I have lived through without what God gave through Agnes and also what He gave as a result of her teaching how to hear Him.

I could not have made it: Without the Natural and the Spiritual flowing together... Without Jesus bringing us back to the Father... Without His Be-Attitudes. I would have never been in my right mind without the revelation of Isaiah 26, and how God Himself, made us a new creature, free from the former lords.

As I travel around the world, I see pastors and leaders

struggle with what to teach their people. Maybe they have never had Bible School training... and may never be able to afford it.

I appreciate the opportunity to have lived this life changing experience and now, thousands of hours, many authors, editors, artists and volunteers later we are offering this simple Gospel to the world.

We realize this is the first edition. We are still making videos to go along with the teaching. It is simple because Rev. Agnes always ministered the simple, yet profound truth of the Gospel.

Our cry is that God will read this to you... that He will impart His Gospel to your heart and that He will train you, that you will experience the freedom, peace power and ability to demonstrate His Love to the Nations.

May we all work together while there is time.... That He alone may be glorified.

"And this gospel of the kingdom shall be preached in all the world for a witness unto all nations; and then shall the end come." Matthew 24:14

Let Jesus take you to the Nations.....

Teresa Skinner

Project Director

facebook.com/AllNationsIs58
twitter.com/AllNationsIs58
instagram.com/AllNationsIs58
amazon.com/author/teresaskinner

www.ingramcontent.com/pod-product-compliance
Lightning Source LLC
Chambersburg PA
CBHW052152110526
44591CB00012B/1951